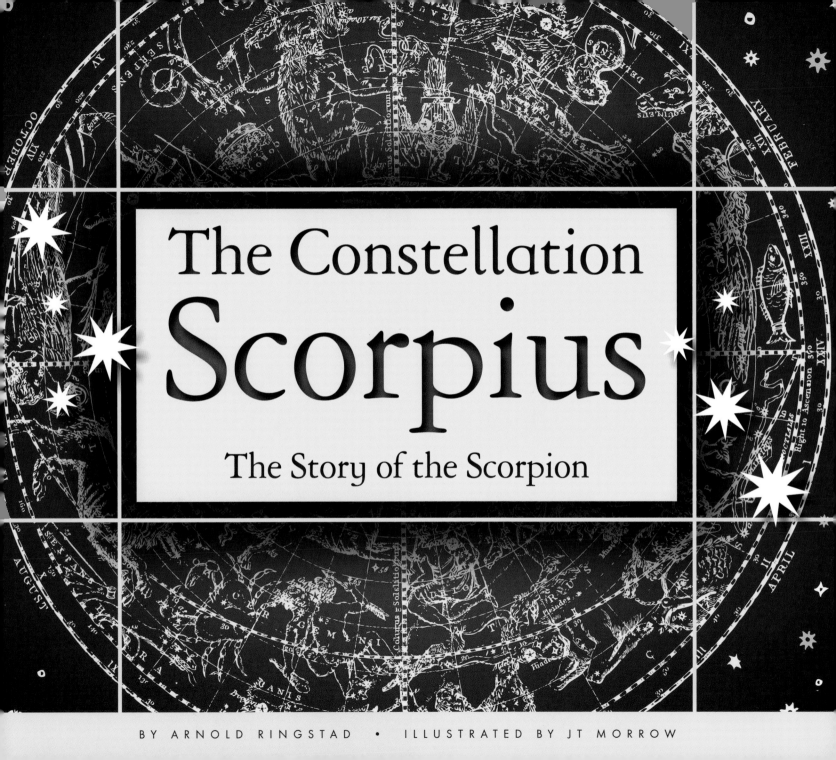

The Constellation
Scorpius
The Story of the Scorpion

BY ARNOLD RINGSTAD • ILLUSTRATED BY JT MORROW

The Child's World

Published by The Child's World®
1980 Lookout Drive • Mankato, MN 56003-1705
800-599-READ • www.childsworld.com

Acknowledgments
The Child's World®: Mary Berendes, Publishing Director
Red Line Editorial: Editorial direction and production
The Design Lab: Design

Photographs ©: Sergey Mikhaylov/Shutterstock Images, 5; NASA, 6,
11; inigo cia/Shutterstock Images, 7; Lisa Yen/Shutterstock Images,
8; Thomas Tuchan/iStockphoto, 9; ESA/NASA, 10; DEA/G. DAGLI
ORTI/Getty Images, 13; Classix/iStockphoto, 14; Vydunas/Shutterstock
Images, 15; Library of Congress, 17; Ryszard Stelmachowicz/
Shutterstock Images, 25

Design elements: Alisafoytik/Dreamstime

ISBN: 9781623234881
LCCN: 2013931359

Printed in the United States of America
Mankato, MN
November, 2014
PA02251

ABOUT THE AUTHOR
Arnold Ringstad lives in Minnesota.
He loves looking into the night sky with
his telescope.

ABOUT THE ILLUSTRATOR
JT Morrow has worked as a freelance
illustrator for more than 20 years and has
won several awards. He also works in
graphic design and animation. Morrow
lives just south of San Francisco, California,
with his wife and daughter.

Table of Contents

CHAPTER 1

The Constellation Scorpius

A deadly scorpion lurks in the night sky. The stinger on its tail is ready to strike. It is easy to find if you know where to look. It is a constellation.

A bright red star is at its center. A line of dimmer stars curves away behind it. They make up its tail. Groups of stars stick out to the sides. They make eight legs. More stars reach forward. They create its fierce **pincers**. This night-sky scorpion is known as Scorpius.

What Is a Constellation?

Scorpius is one of many constellations. Constellations are groups of stars that create shapes and figures in the sky. People connected the dots to make the first constellations thousands of years ago.

▼ Stars in Scorpius form its stinger, tail, body, and pincers.

The shapes organized the vast night sky. People saw the shapes as characters from their culture. The scorpion Scorpius comes from ancient Greek **mythology**.

What Is a Star?

Stars are enormous balls of gas. They release tremendous amounts of energy. They send out the energy as heat and light. The Sun is the most familiar star. The Sun is medium sized compared to other stars. However, it is huge compared to the planets in our solar system. It weighs 743 times more than all the planets combined.

We can see thousands of stars in the sky on a clear night. However, these are a tiny fraction of all stars. Scientists think there may be

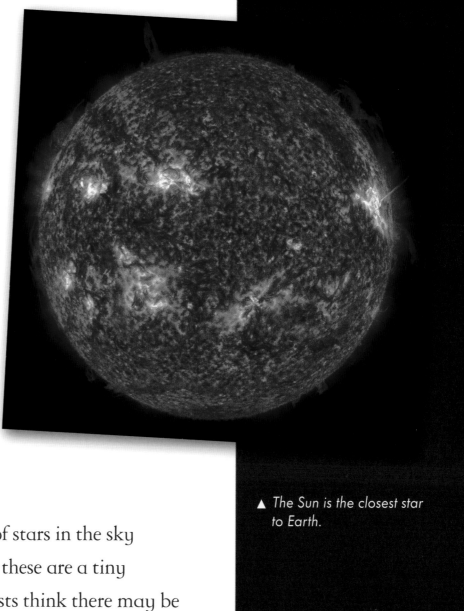

▲ The Sun is the closest star to Earth.

300,000,000,000,000,000,000,000 (300 sextillion) stars in the **universe**! That could be 40,000 times as many stars as there are grains of sand in all the beaches and deserts on Earth.

Stars are also incredibly far away from us. Our fastest spacecraft would take 80,000 years to reach the closest star, Proxima Centauri.

▼ *The stars we see from Earth are only a tiny percentage of all stars in the universe.*

Stars in Scorpius

The brightest star in Scorpius is at its center. This star is called Antares. The enormous Antares is bright red. It is approximately 700 times larger than our Sun and 10,000 times brighter. It is the 15th-brightest star in the night sky. Antares has a second star nearby. This star, Antares B, is much fainter. Usually you need a large telescope to see it from Earth.

▲ Stars in Scorpius

ANTARES

Antares's name probably comes from a Greek phrase. The phrase translates to "rival of Ares." Ares is another name for Mars. The planet Mars is also bright and red. The ancient Greeks may have seen Antares and Mars as competitors.

The stars Shaula and Lesath are located at the scorpion's stinger. Shaula is a brilliant star. It is the 21st-brightest of all visible stars. The star system Graffias is at Scorpius's head. Graffias has at least five stars tightly circling each other.

▶ In this zoomed-in look at Scorpius, Antares is the bright orange star to the left.

Deep-Sky Objects

There are several deep-sky objects in Scorpius. A deep-sky object is something outside our solar system that isn't a star. Examples include clusters of stars and even whole **galaxies**. There are four important deep-sky objects in Scorpius. They belong to a group known as Messier objects. These are named after their discoverer, French **astronomer** Charles Messier.

Two of the Messier objects are bright **star clusters** called M6 and M7. A star cluster's stars are packed tightly together. M6 and M7 are both found near the scorpion's tail. They are visible without a telescope on dark, clear nights. The star cluster M4 is near Scorpius's central star. It is smaller and fainter than M6 and M7. You can see it with a small telescope. M80 is the fourth Messier object. This large but faint star cluster lies near the scorpion's pincers.

▲ *The powerful space telescope Hubble took this image inside the M4 star cluster.*

YOU LIVE IN A STAR CLUSTER
Our own Sun itself is actually part of a star cluster. This means that you live in the middle of a star cluster! The cluster also includes the nearby star system Alpha Centauri. It was formed about 5 billion years ago. There are about 20,000 other clusters like it inside our galaxy.

▶ *Opposite page: In our cosmic neighborhood, the Sun is near Alpha Centauri.*

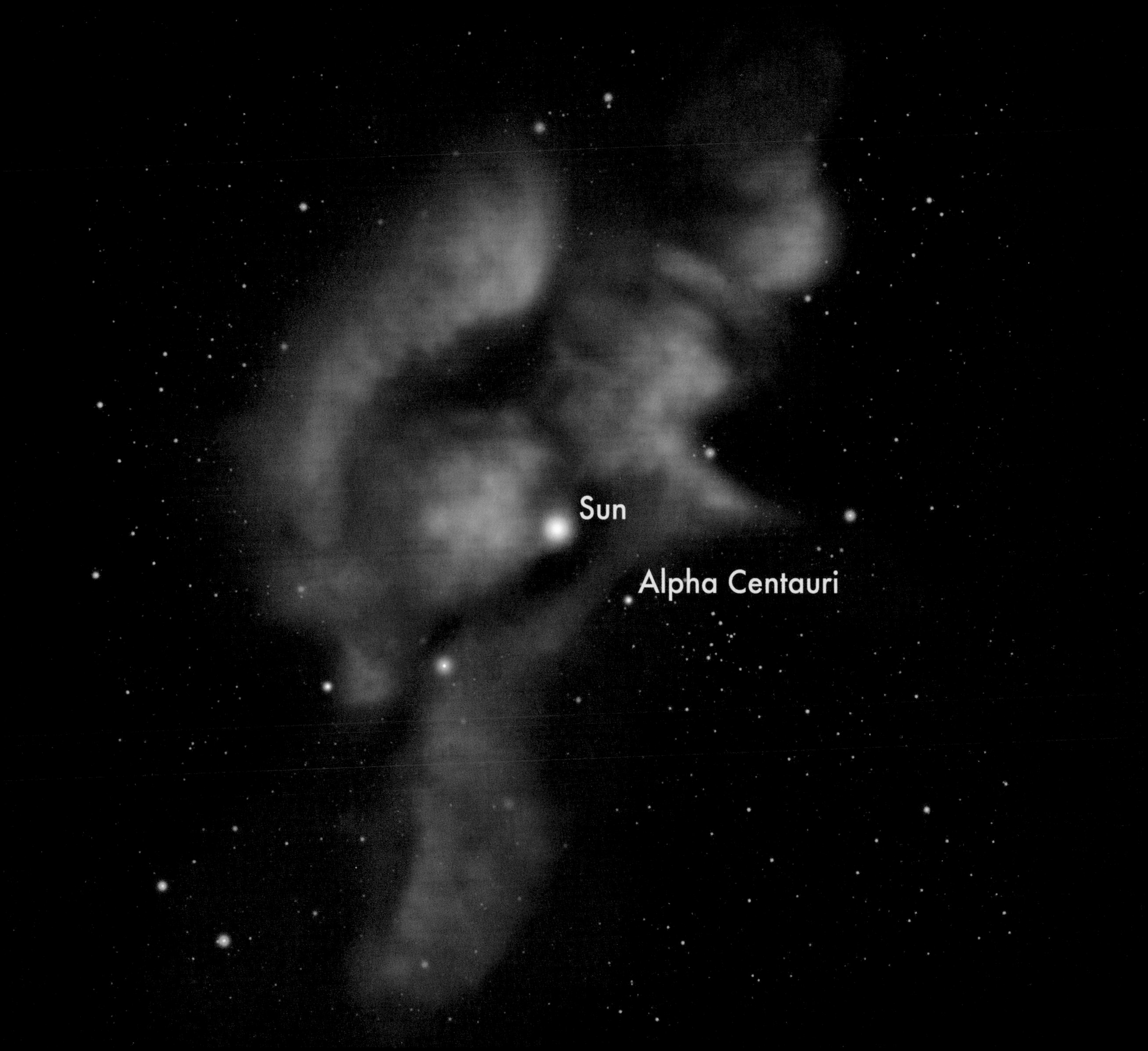
Sun
Alpha Centauri

CHAPTER 2

The Origin of the Myth of Scorpius

The constellation Scorpius dates back to ancient **Mesopotamia**. Descriptions and images of it on stone tablets are 3,000 years old. It was originally a symbol of darkness and bravery.

Scorpius appears during the middle of the summer. The days get shorter soon after it appears. Ancient people, including the Mesopotamians, connected these two events. The constellation became a symbol of the coming of autumn. It represented the

► *Opposite page: The scorpion appeared in ancient Mesopotamian art and religion*

fading power of the Sun. The Mesopotamians' story of the scorpion was passed down to the ancient Greeks along with many other constellations.

ASTROLOGY

Some people believe a person's **zodiac** sign influences his or her personality. For instance, some say Scorpios are happy around other people but hold many secrets. The belief in this connection between signs and personalities is called astrology. Scientists have not found evidence that astrology is true.

◀ *The 12 signs of the zodiac*

Ancient astronomers divided the sky into 12 equal slices. The division is called the zodiac. Each slice is named after one of its constellations. The slices are commonly called signs of the zodiac. The slice containing Scorpius is known as the sign of the scorpion. Because the zodiac divides the sky into different parts, the signs can also be used to tell the locations of objects such as planets.

The zodiac also divides the calendar year into 12 parts. This division is based on when the Sun passes through each slice of sky. Many people use the zodiac in this way today. People born between October 23 and November 21 are called Scorpios. They are said to be born under the sign of the scorpion.

▼ Scorpions have long been respected for their deadly beauty.

Scorpius and Libra

Scorpius was one of the ancient Greeks' largest constellations. It originally had enormous pincers. Eventually, Scorpius's pincers became much smaller. Those stars became the constellation Libra. Libra looks like a set of weighing scales representing justice and fairness.

Around the year 150, the Greek astronomer Ptolemy wrote a book about astronomy. It contained all of his knowledge of the skies. The book listed more than 1,000 stars. They were divided into 48 constellations. Today, there are 88 constellations. Scorpius was one of Ptolemy's original 48 constellations.

THE 88 CONSTELLATIONS
Ptolemy created his list of constellations more than 1,800 years ago. But the modern set of 88 constellations wasn't complete until 1922. Many constellations were added in the 1600s and 1700s. Astronomers filled in the sky of the Southern Hemisphere. They completed the last few gaps in the northern sky. By the 1800s, a book listed more than 100 constellations. Later astronomers decided there were too many constellations. The final set of 88 was officially accepted in 1922.

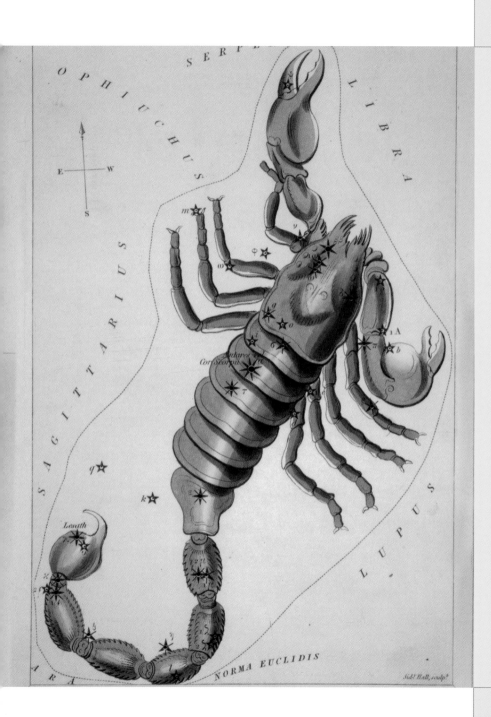

CHAPTER 3

The Story of Scorpius

There are several versions of the story of Scorpius. Most of them include the scorpion's connection to another figure from Greek mythology, the mighty hunter and warrior Orion. Scorpius and Orion are always deadly enemies.

The Greek writer Aratus tells one version of the story. As he tells it, one day Orion fell in love with the goddess Artemis. He chased her. He refused to leave her alone and would not stop bothering her.

Finally, Artemis became frustrated. Artemis was the goddess of the hunt. She had power over all animals. She summoned a tiny scorpion and sent it after Orion. Orion was a mighty hunter. But he was no match for the little scorpion. The scorpion found him, stung him, and killed him.

Other Greek writers tell the story differently. In their stories, Orion and Artemis were friends. They hunted together. Orion believed he was the greatest hunter ever. He made a boast to Artemis. He said he could kill any animal in the world. This made the Earth goddess Gaia angry.

Gaia opened a huge crack in the ground. Out of the crack rushed a giant scorpion. Moving quicker than lightning, it stung Orion. The poisonous sting killed him.

After Orion died, Artemis felt pity for him. She prayed to Zeus to honor Orion. Zeus was the king of the gods and Artemis's father.

Zeus made Scorpius a constellation. He wanted to warn people not to be too boastful. He also saw Artemis's love for Orion. So he placed Orion in the sky to honor his skill and courage.

Zeus put Orion and Scorpius on opposite sides of the sky. This would keep the two fighting constellations apart. Orion always falls below the horizon as Scorpius rises. Orion is always running away from Scorpius, even in the night sky.

ZEUS
Zeus was the king of the Greek gods. The ancient Greeks believed his home was atop Mount Olympus. He watched over all humans and gods. Zeus controlled the wind, rain, and storms. His weapon was the mighty thunderbolt. Zeus was the father of many other gods, including Artemis, Apollo, and Athena. In Greek mythology, Zeus placed many of the constellations in the sky. These include Scorpius, Orion, and Gemini.

CHAPTER 4

Scorpius in Other Cultures

China

In ancient China, the stars in Scorpius made different constellations. Antares was called Huo. This star was the heart of the Blue Dragon constellation. The stars forming the scorpion's head make the dragon's body. The stars in Scorpius's tail make the dragon's tail.

To the right of the tail are 12 stars. They form a group of soldiers ready to defend against invaders. Six of these stars belong to Scorpius. The other six belong to nearby constellations. To the left of the tail is Yu, a fish swimming through the Milky Way. Yu is represented by the deep-sky object M7.

Tahiti

The Polynesians of Tahiti have another story for the stars in Scorpius. In the story, two small children run away from home. The children are brother and sister. They run far, far away. Finally they come to an enormous hill. The climb up the hill is long and difficult. The children are exhausted when they reach the top. At the top, they lay down and begin to cry.

Soon their parents realize the children are gone. The parents quickly start to search for them. They find faint footprints from the children. They follow the footprints all the way to the hill. They begin to climb the hill to get their children back.

The children see their parents coming and panic. They do not want to go home. They find a giant stag beetle on the hill. They ask him to help them escape. He agrees and tells the children to climb onto his back. Then he leaps high, high into the air.

The parents look up to see their children flying away into the night sky. The beetle returns to its home in Antares. The two children become the two bright stars in the tail of Scorpius.

CHAPTER 5

How to Find Scorpius

The easiest way to find Scorpius is to locate its brightest star, Antares. In the Northern **Hemisphere**, look low in the southern sky to find it. It is most visible in the early summer. Its brightness and its reddish color make it easy to find. Antares has two stars very near to it on either side. Together these stars make up the heart of the scorpion.

SCORPIUS'S TAIL AND PINCERS

From Antares, look for the line of stars that moves away from it to the lower left. The line then curves in a clockwise direction. These are the stars that make up the tail. Two bright stars are right next to each other at the end of the tail. They create Scorpius's stinger. Finally, look just to the right of Antares. Find the short line of stars that runs up and down. These stars form the pincers of Scorpius, the fearsome scorpion that lurks in the night sky.

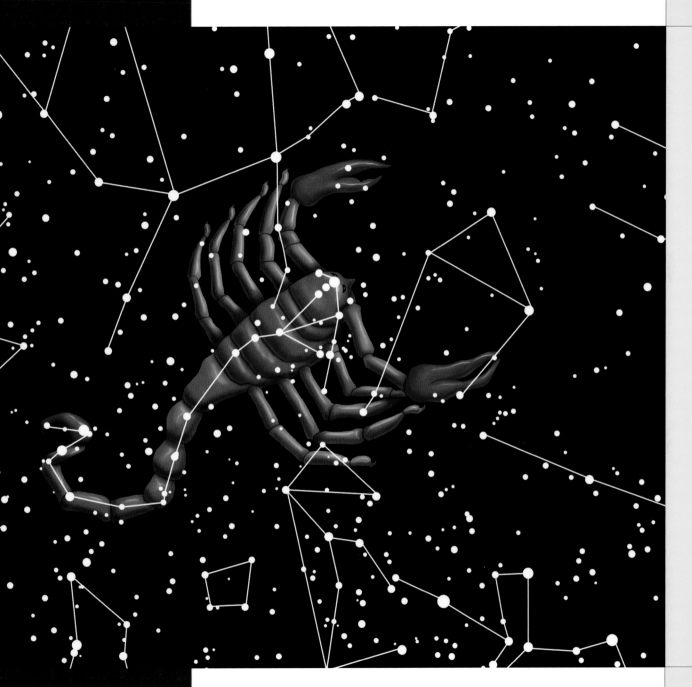

Glossary

astronomer (uh-STRAW-nuh-mur)
A scientist who studies stars and other objects in space is called an astronomer. The astronomer discovered a new star.

galaxies (GAL-ax-eez)
Groups of millions or billions of stars form galaxies. Some bright lights in the night sky are galaxies.

hemisphere (HEM-uh-spheer)
One half of a planet is one hemisphere. You can see Scorpius from the Northern Hemisphere.

Mesopotamia (meh-sah-poh-TAY-mee-ah)
The area of ancient Mesopotamia is now Iraq, Syria, and Turkey. The Mesopotamians studied the stars.

mythology (mith-AH-luh-jee)
Mythology is a culture's set of stories or beliefs. Zeus is a god from Greek mythology.

pincers (PIN-sers)
Pincers are the front claws of animals such as scorpions, lobsters, or crabs. Stars in the constellation Scorpius stand for the scorpion's pincers.

star clusters (STAR clus-tuhrs)
Star clusters are closely packed groups of stars within a galaxy. Several star clusters lie in the constellation Scorpius.

universe (YOU-nih-verse)
The universe is everything that exists in space. The universe is huge and filled with stars.

zodiac (ZOH-dee-ak)
The zodiac is an imaginary circle with 12 wedges that divide the sky. Scorpius is a sign of the zodiac.

Learn More

Books

Heifetz, Milton D., and Wil Tirion. *A Walk through the Heavens: A Guide to Stars and Constellations and Their Legends*. New York: Cambridge University Press, 1996.

Otfinoski, Steven. *Mythlopedia: All in the Family: A Look-It-Up Guide to the In-laws, Outlaws, and Offspring of Mythology*. New York: Scholastic, 2007.

Ridpath, Ian. *Eyewitness Companions: Astronomy*. New York: DK Publishing, 2006.

Web Sites

Visit our Web site for links about Scorpius:

childsworld.com/links

Note to Parents, Teachers, and Librarians:
We routinely verify our Web links to make sure they are safe and active sites.
So encourage your readers to check them out!

Index